Contents

First published in the UK in 2001 by Red Kite,

an imprint of Haldane Mason Ltd, 59 Chepstow Road, London W2 5BP. email: haldane.mason@dial.pipex.com

Copyright © Haldane Mason Ltd, 2001

ISBN: 1-902463-28-5

A HALDANE MASON BOOK

Editor: Ambreen Husain **Designer**: Rachel Clark **Illustrators**: Phil Ford & Stephen Dew **Educational Consultant**: John Stringer BSc

Colour reproduction by CK Litho Ltd, UK Printed in the UAE

Picture Acknowledgements

AQUAPARK di Zambrone 23; **Bruce Coleman Collection** /Andrew Purcell 29; **courtesy of Ford Motor Company Ltd** 7; **Image Bank** 5, /Terje Rakke 22, /Alan Becker 26; **Mary Evans Picture Library** 8, 10, 25; **Powergen UK plc** 30; **Science Photo Library** 14, /Sheila Terry 17, /NASA 21.

Note: The experiments described in this book are designed to be safe and easy to carry out at home. The author and publishers can accept no responsibility for any accidents that occur as a result of using the book. If in doubt, consult an adult.

Family of Forces

This book is about electricity and forces. Everyone knows about electricity. It's the stuff that makes bulbs light up and computers work. And forces? They're something to do with pushing and pulling. If that sounds a bit dull and a bit vague, it soon won't be. The next few pages will reveal the fascinating facts about shocking static, magical magnetism, gripping gravity, and much more. And you'll be able to try out lots of things yourself. But, before all that, a quick tour of the world of electricity and forces to see what links them together.

The big link

Let's think about energy first of all. Energy makes things happen or does work. It comes in lots of different forms. Whenever something happens, one kind of energy changes to another kind. When you jump in the air, you're changing chemical energy – stored in your body from food you've eaten – to kinetic – movement – energy. Electrical energy becomes heat energy when an electric heater is switched on.

Whenever energy is used, forces are involved. And electricity is a form of energy. That's the link. Forces hold things together, break them apart, start or stop things moving, change their direction, or bend and twist them. Some very bright physicists – scientists who work out how the world works – have, over the years, found out that there are just four basic forces in the Universe that hold everything together: gravity, electromagnetic force, the force between the particles that make up atoms, and the sort of nuclear forces from which the Sun's heat and light comes. All other forces arise from these basic forces.

The important thing is that, without energy and forces, nothing would happen anywhere in the Universe – the Sun wouldn't shine, the wind wouldn't blow and there wouldn't be any TV to watch.

Powerful winds, such as this tornado, happen because of energy and forces.

4

mad about science

...ricity

...rces

Consultant: John Stringer BSc

ReD

Welcome to Mad About Science: Electricity & Forces!

Discover the amazing facts about shocking static, mysterious magnetism and gripping gravity, with fascinating experiments you can try at home. Science has never been so much fun!

The pages are packed with colourful illustrations, useful information and incredible facts. You'll meet the 'father of electricity', learn how electricity gets from one place to another, find out why ships float and stones sink, and why you would immediately be squashed flat in the deepest part of the ocean.

Throughout the book, you will find experiments that are fun and easy to do. You'll find most of the things you need for them in your home. You can get other items, such as insulated wire and bulbs in bulb holders, from shops that sell electrical supplies. Look up your nearest one in your local phone book. Follow the instructions for each experiment carefully and always take care with sharp tools and electrical equipment. Never experiment with mains electricity.

If you want to find a particular subject, just look it up in the index at the back. Otherwise, simply turn to page 4 and let the fun begin!

Did you know?

The Sun is responsible for that strong wind that sent your hat flying down the street. Heat from the Sun warms the air around the Earth and makes it rise. Cold air sinks and fills the gap left. This movement of air forms the winds that provide a force to push trees and people. Wind power can be useful, too – it can be used to turn generators that produce electricity.

Generators produce the electricity that brings heat and light to our homes and offices.

Try this!

A day's work

Make a list of all the ways in which forces (pushes, pulls, twists and turns) and electricity play a part in one day of your life.

Did you know?

▶▶ Magnetism and electricity are closely related because magnets are used to make electricity, and electricity can be used to make magnets.

▶▶ Pliers, nutcrackers, and hammers are all examples of simple machines – devices that allow you to apply a greater force than would normally be possible to get things done.

▶▶ Gravity is a weak force compared to others, but it's strong enough to keep your feet on the ground and make the tides work.

5

Amazing fact

You use energy and forces to run. How fast are you moving at the moment? Have a guess. You might be surprised to know that the ground beneath your feet is whirling round the Sun at an incredible 100,000 kmh.

Earliest Electricity

Unless you are in the middle of nowhere and without a power supply, you're sure to be using electricity in some form. From providing light to running a computer, electricity is an important part of our everyday lives. Surprisingly, we haven't been using it for very long. Ancient civilizations knew bits and pieces about it but no one took any real interest in electricity until the 18th century.

Ecstatic about static

Ancient Greek philosopher Thales of Miletus (624–545 BC) made the first breakthrough when he discovered that a piece of amber – a bit of fossilized tree resin – would pick up feathers after it was rubbed with fur. About 2,200 years later (things moved more slowly in those days) physician William Gilbert – the star of page 12 – showed that what happened to amber also happened to glass. He called this strange force of attraction 'electricity' after 'elektron', the Greek word for amber. Today we call electricity produced by rubbing two objects together static electricity – electricity that does not flow. Why does it happen? Everything in the Universe is made up of tiny particles called atoms. Atoms have even tinier particles inside them – whizzing round a

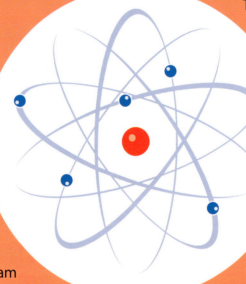

All atoms have a central part called the nucleus, which has a positive charge. Negatively-charged electrons constantly spin around the nucleus.

central nucleus are minute electrons. The nucleus has a positive electrical charge and the electrons have a negative charge. When two objects, or materials, rub together – like fur and amber – electrons are knocked off the atoms of one and stick on to the atoms of the other. This gives one of them – the one with the extra electrons – a negative charge, and the other one a positive charge. Two objects with opposite charges attract, and those with the same charge repel.

Some materials, such as metals, will lose electrons easily, allowing electricity to pass through them. They are conductors. Other materials, such as glass and amber, will not let electricity pass through them, but they do become electrically charged. They are called insulators.

6

Try this!

Static attraction

Take some lightweight paper – toilet paper is good for this – and tear it up into tiny pieces. Next, rub an ordinary plastic ball-point pen with a piece of cloth for about 30 seconds. Then hold the pen near the shredded paper. It will pick up the pieces. Why? Because rubbing the plastic with the cloth has given it an electrical charge, so it attracts the paper.

Amazing fact

Factories use static to do a really good paint job. The item to be painted is given one charge and the paint is given another. The two attract each other and the paint 'jumps' into place.

Try this!

Charged balloons

Put on a jumper and then blow up two balloons. Rub one against your jumper. Now hold it close to you. It will 'stick' to your jumper because the negatively-charged balloon is attracted to the positively-charged jumper. Now rub both the balloons against your jumper. Then hold them by their tied ends and bring them close to each other. They should push away from each other. Why? Because both are now negatively-charged, and like charges repel.

Did you know?

Stephen Gray (1666–1736) showed that the human body conducts electricity in a rather unusual way. He took a poor boy from the streets and suspended him above the ground by his arms and legs using silk threads. He got his housekeeper to rub the boy's clothes with a glass rod. Then Gray told the boy to reach towards the ground where there were lots of pieces of paper. Amazingly, the paper flew up towards the boy's fingers. The glass rod had removed electrons from his clothes, giving them a positive charge, and this had passed through to his skin. Once charged, the skin attracted the scraps of paper without the boy touching them.

7

Lightning Strike

Thunderstorms are pretty scary things, but at least scientists understand what's making the bangs and flashes. But thousands, even hundreds, of years ago, you would have been scared for good reason. Greeks, Romans and Vikings all thought storms were sent by powerful gods. If you were really unlucky you might be struck by a thunderbolt from an angry god who was having an off day. Bright spark Benjamin Franklin changed all this.

Benjamin's brainstorm

An American inventor, scientist, and statesman, Benjamin Franklin (1706–1790) was fascinated by electricity. He had seen Leyden jars that were used to store static electricity, and was interested by the spark that leapt from the globe on top of the jars to a piece of metal or a hand placed nearby.

As he watched this happen, he had a bright idea: perhaps lightning was actually just a big spark. He decided to test his idea, even though he knew it would be dangerous.

It was 1752. Franklin chose a rainy day with a thunderstorm looming on the horizon. Taking a huge risk, he flew a kite with a metal wire sticking out of it. Near his end of the string, which was wet because of the rain, was a key. Standing in a wooden shed to keep himself dry, Franklin held on to the kite string with a piece of dry silk, which would not carry electricity. When lightning flashed he put his hand near the key and something remarkable happened. Sparks leapt to his hand and he received a shock.

So that was it – lightning was definitely just a great big spark.

Benjamin Franklin risked his life when he flew a kite in a thunderstorm, but he made a remarkable discovery.

Did you know?

In storm clouds, water droplets and ice rub together and become charged. The top of the cloud has a positive charge and the bottom has a negative charge. The ground below has a positive charge. Eventually the electricity discharges from the cloud to the ground and back again (forked lightning) or inside the cloud (sheet lightning). This big spark heats up the air around it which expands explosively with a noise called thunder.

When the electrical charges in the cloud and the ground are large enough, the electricity discharges to the ground and we see a flash of lightning.

Did you know?

▶▶ Ben Franklin's kite experiment made people really start thinking seriously about electricity. He kept thinking about it, too – in 1753, Franklin invented the lightning conductor, a device that protects buildings from lightning strikes. It is still used today.

▶▶ Researchers who copied Benjamin Franklin's experiments were not all as fortunate as he was. Georg Richmann of St Petersburg, Russia, erected a wire-tipped pole in a storm and got a massive shock that killed him outright.

9

Try this!

Making sparks

You can make your own electricity sparks at home. Wearing a T-shirt, take an ordinary blown-up balloon and a radio into a darkened room. Rub the balloon against your T-shirt so that it becomes charged. Now look carefully as you hold it close to the aerial of the radio. You should see tiny sparks – like mini-flashes of lightning – as negative charges jump from the balloon to the aerial.

Stay in the dark room and get a friend to help you. They should wear a jumper. Ask your friend to take off and put on their jumper. When it rubs against the rest of their clothes, you should see tiny sparks – and you may be able to hear a crackling sound as the electricity discharges.

Current Provider

By the 18th century scientists could make static electricity, but they couldn't do much with it, apart from storing it or discharging it in an instant. They didn't know that electricity could move as a continuous stream of electrons called current. Two things were needed: an unbroken path for the current to travel along, and a way of producing a constant supply of electricity to keep the current flowing. It took two Italians, one dead frog, and an argument to put these two things together.

How Volta made his pile

Luigi Galvani (1737–1798) and Alessandro Volta (1745–1827) were both excited about electricity. Galvani noticed that when he touched a dead frog lying on a brass plate with a metal scalpel, the frog's legs twitched. Galvani declared that there was 'animal electricity' in frogs' muscles. Volta disagreed. He said that the two different metals – of the plate and the scalpel – reacted with liquid inside the muscles to produce electricity and make the muscles twitch. They couldn't agree, so Volta decided to prove his idea. He took two metal discs and put a paper disc soaked in salt solution between them. He linked a wire to each metal disc and touched the free ends to his tongue. The tingle he felt told him he had made electricity! Volta then discovered that if he piled up these three-disc units, he could produce more electricity than with one.

Volta's pile was the forerunner of the modern battery.

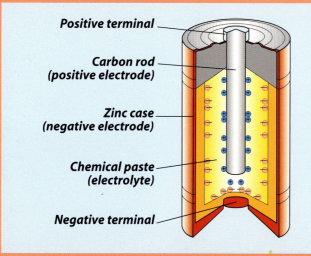

Positive terminal

Carbon rod
(positive electrode)

Zinc case
(negative electrode)

Chemical paste
(electrolyte)

Negative terminal

Did you know?

The earliest batteries – or cells, as they are known – consisted of two different metals, called electrodes, with liquids, especially acids, as the electrolyte. The batteries we use today are called dry cells because they don't contain any liquid sloshing around. This makes them very portable – just the thing for torches and personal stereos. They still have two electrodes – a carbon one in the middle and a zinc one in the casing. The electrolyte is a chemical paste.

Try this! Lemon battery

You can use a lemon to make a simple battery. You will need two pieces of insulated wire with clips, a copper coin, a galvanized – zinc-covered – nail, and some fine sandpaper. Ask an adult to make two small slits in the lemon. Shine the coin and the nail with the sandpaper. Now stick the coin into one slit and the nail into the other. Clip the wires to the coin and the nail. Touch the other ends of the wires to your tongue. You should feel a tingle – the lemon battery is making electricity, and a current is flowing through the wires and your tongue. Why does it work? The zinc reacts with the acidic lemon juice – the electrolyte – and loses positive charge, so it has an excess of negative charge. This excess moves along the wire as an electric current through your tongue to the copper coin.

Round the circuit

It's easy to get electricity to where you need it because it flows straight there along wires. When a force is provided by a source of electrical energy, like a battery, the electrons in a wire are pushed along by the electrons from the source – both have negative charges – and nudged into atoms further along the wire. As electrons are nudged from atom to atom, the charge is carried along the wire. This will only happen if there is an unbroken path between the negative and positive terminals of the battery or source of electrical energy. This path is called the electrical circuit and can include wires, light bulbs, and any other bits. A switch is used to break the circuit or to make it. You've probably noticed that electrical wires have a plastic covering. Plastic is an insulator, ensuring that electricity does not pass out of the wire – so it's safe for you to hold.

11

Try this! Making a circuit

You will need a 1.5 volt battery, two insulated wires with clips, and a bulb in a bulb holder. Clip one end of each wire to the bulb holder. Now hold the other end of each wire to one of the terminals – positive or negative – of the battery. As you make the circuit, current flows along the wire from the negative end of the battery to the positive, and the bulb lights up. Take the wire away from one of the terminals. The bulb will go out because you've broken the circuit.

The Big Attraction

Have you noticed how many people have fridge magnets these days? Perhaps you have some yourself. They can hold shopping lists or favourite photos on display, seemingly by magic. But, what is actually doing the holding is not magic but an invisible force called a magnetic field. Magnets attract iron and some other metals. They also attract or repel (push away) other magnets. All magnets have two ends called north and south poles. It's at these poles that magnetic forces are strongest.

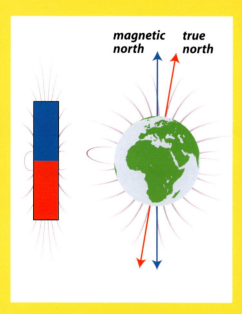

magnetic north   true north

12

One big magnet

There is a story that, around 2500 BC, a Chinese emperor led his troops through a thick fog using a piece of rock dangling from a thread. This wasn't any old rock, though. It was a piece of lodestone, a rock that contains magnetite and is naturally magnetic. Although people knew that a piece of dangling lodestone would point North to South, no-one knew why it worked until along came William Gilbert (1544–1603), physician to Queen Elizabeth I. Gilbert experimented with a magnetized needle and found that the North-pointing end of his needle also dipped downwards. His conclusion? That the Earth was one big magnet with north and south magnetic poles.

Amazing fact

Doctors can use small electromagnets to pull metal splinters straight out of a person's eyes, quickly and painlessly, without causing any other damage.

Try this! Opposites attract

Take two bar magnets. Put one on a table. Push the south pole of the second magnet towards the south pole of the first. The first magnet will move away from the second. Now push the north pole towards the south. The magnets should clang together. Why? Because like poles repel and unlike poles attract.

Pulling power

Electricity and magnetism are closely linked. Take a wire, put an electric current through it and the current produces a magnetic field around the wire. In 1820 Hans Christian Oersted (1777–1851), a Danish scientist, happened to place a compass near a wire carrying electricity. The compass needle moved to line up with the wire – and he discovered electromagnetism.

Electromagnets are made by passing a current through coiled wire, as the magnetic effect is much stronger than with a straight wire. The electromagnet can be made even stronger by putting an iron rod down the middle of it. And it can be switched on and off.

By 1830, electromagnets were strong enough to lift pieces of iron weighing about 5kg. In the United States, engineer and inventor Joseph Henry (1797–1878) covered the wire with silk before coiling it. This insulated the wire so that current could not short-circuit (jump from loop to loop rather than pass along the wire). So he could pack more loops into his coil – so many that his improved electromagnet could lift 340kg.

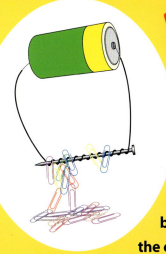

Try this!
Make your own electromagnet

You will need a long piece of insulated copper wire, a 1.5v battery, a large nail, and some paper clips. Wrap the wire around a pencil to make loops, with enough loose wire at each end to reach the battery. Move the coil of wire near the paper clips. Now make a circuit by touching the two ends of the wire to each end of the battery. Can you pick up the paper clips? Don't hold the wire for long as it will get hot very quickly. To boost the magnetic field, slip the nail into the middle of the coil and make the circuit again. How many do you pick up this time?

13

Did you know?

Electromagnets do much more than lifting. They are used in loudspeakers, intruder alarms, metal detectors at airports and many other things. One everyday example is the doorbell. When you press the bell push you complete a circuit. A current flows through the circuit, and switches on an electromagnet inside the bell. It attracts an iron arm with a hammer at the end. As the arm moves, the hammer strikes the bell and makes a sound. When the hammer strikes, it breaks the circuit and, as the electromagnet is switched off, the arm springs back to its original position. There, of course, it makes the circuit again so the hammer hits the bell. This repeated action happens rapidly so what you hear is the continuous ringing of the bell (until you take your finger off the bell push).

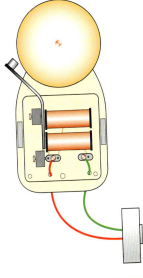

Power for People

Not only is it easy to get it where you want it but, as a kind of energy, electricity is so easily turned into other types of energy. Look at a light bulb, converting electrical energy into light. Or a hairdryer, converting it into heat. Hairdryers, washing machines, video recorders, and lots of other everyday things that we take for granted all have something in common. They do what they do because they are powered by electric motors.

Motor power

English scientist Michael Faraday (1791-1867) realized that electricity and magnetism could be used to make things move. His first apparatus consisted of a bar magnet fixed in a bowl of mercury – a liquid metal that conducted electricity – and a loop of wire suspended around the magnet. When he sent an electric current down the wire, it started to rotate around the magnet. Faraday had made the first basic electric motor.

Because of his work, Michael Faraday became known as the 'father of electricity'.

During the decades that followed, scientists and inventors developed on Faraday's work and eventually produced the first practical working motors. In a simple electric motor, current is provided by a battery and flows through a coil that is between the north and south poles of a magnet. As current flows through the coil, a magnetic field is produced around it. This reacts to the magnetic field of the magnet and makes the coil turn. When the coil has made a half-turn, its magnetic field will match the magnet's so it will stop turning. But a device called a commutator ensures that the coil keeps turning, by reversing the current every half-turn. The continuous turning motion of the coil is what drives the motor.

14

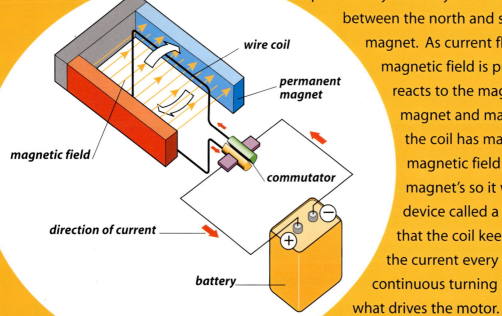

wire coil

permanent magnet

magnetic field

commutator

direction of current

battery

Generation game

In 1831, Faraday had another bright idea – if electricity and a magnet could make a coil move, perhaps a moving magnet and a coil would produce electricity. So he tried moving a magnet inside a coil of wire. And it worked – he had 'generated' electricity by 'inducing' a current in the wire. Faraday's discovery led to the development of the generators that provide electricity for our homes and for factories and offices.

Amazing fact

Electricity is used to restart people's hearts if they stop working. If their heart stops, a person cannot survive very long. Fortunately, in some cases, a sudden electric shock restarts the heart's own electrical activity.

Did you know?

▶▶ Cars use electric motors to start their petrol or diesel-powered engines. But electrically-powered cars are still in development. One of the problems is that the batteries needed to power an electric car over a long journey would be too big to fit inside it. Until a different kind of battery is developed, an electric car won't take you far.

▶▶ Thomas Edison (1847-1931) invented the first electric light bulb, and then went on to develop the first electricity meter, so that people could be charged for the electricity they used.

15

Try this!

Make your own generator

You will need two long pieces of insulated copper wire with clips at each end, a bar magnet, a compass and a friend to help you. Wrap one piece of copper wire round a pencil to make a coil (as you did on page 13). Make a loop in the other piece of wire and ask your friend to hold it near the compass. Connect the two pieces of wire with the clips. Next, tie a piece of string round one end of the bar magnet. Now start generating. Move the magnet quickly up and down inside the coil of wire. You should see the compass needle moving. Why? Because moving the magnet inside the coil induces an electric current in the wire. This, in turn, produces a magnetic field around the wire so the needle moves.

On the Move

Movement or motion is going on everywhere, from massive planets zooming round suns to minute particles whizzing about inside atoms. Forces push and pull objects, making them move, change direction, speed up, stop, or even stay exactly where they are. Whack a ball with a bat and the ball flies off into the air – a force has been used to push the ball and make it move in one direction. But forces are not always so straightforward.

Forces at work

Two or more forces – called components – can combine to produce a single force – the resultant – that acts in one direction. When an archer pulls back a bowstring, one component acts up the upper half of the bowstring, and a second along the lower half. The resultant – which is equal and opposite to the pull of the archer's arm – acts forwards along the arrow, so that when the archer lets go, the arrow zings away, straight towards the target.

These combining forces can also make something stay still. In a bridge one component acting downwards – the weight of the bridge plus cars, people and so on – is balanced by the upward push of the towers, arches and cables that support the bridge. The resultant is zero, so the bridge doesn't collapse (engineers have to do some complicated calculations to make sure it doesn't).

Try this!

Support structure

You will need two pieces of paper (about 20 x 30cm in size), some modelling clay or plasticine, and a book. Roll the clay into a ball, then flatten it to make a rectangular base of equal thickness about 6 x 10cm. Roll up the pieces of paper to make tubes about 20cm long and stick them into each end of the clay. Now place the book on top of them. Like a bridge, the tubes of paper push upwards with the same force that the book pushes downwards – they support the book because the forces are balanced.

16

Motion notions

Italian physicist Galileo Galilei (1564–1642) was the first to realize that you don't need a force to keep an object moving – you just need it to start, stop, or accelerate – speed up – the object. Isaac Newton (1642–1727) built on Galileo's ideas, and put forward his three laws of motion that are still used today by scientists to understand how things move.

Newton's work in science was honoured by a knighthood in 1705.

Newton's first law: an object will not move unless it is being pushed or pulled by a force or, if it is moving, it will carry on moving in a straight line at the same speed unless a force acts upon it. Leave this book on the table and it won't move. Give it a shove and it will, but it won't go very far before it stops (unless you shoved it a bit too enthusiastically).

Newton's second law: a force acting on an object will speed it up or slow it down, but the amount of speeding up or slowing down depends on the size of the force and the mass of the object. Push a friend and she or he will move forward, but use the same force on an elephant and … you know the answer.

Newton's third law: if one object pushes or pulls on another object, the second object pushes or pulls back with an equal and opposite force. For every action there is an equal and opposite reaction.

Did you know?

Force is measured in units called newtons (N), named after the great physicist, Sir Isaac Newton. On Earth a mass of 1 kg has a weight – downward force – of 9.8 N. On the Moon, however, its weight would be less (find out why on page 20). Force is measured using a newton meter.

17

Try this!

Get moving

You can see for yourself how Newton's laws of motion work. First, roll a ball – a tennis ball will do – along the ground. The force provided by your arm makes it move, until another force called friction (see page 19) slows it down and eventually stops it. Well done, Newton's first law.

You'll need two balls – of the same size – for the next part. Put one ball in the centre of a large table. Roll the other ball towards it. When the balls collide, the second ball starts to move because it is pushed by the first, and the first ball slows down and changes direction. Try using balls of different sizes. What happens if you roll a football towards a golf ball? Or a tennis ball towards a football? You should see Newton's second law at work.

Next, put on your roller or in-line skates and ask a friend who's the same size as you to do the same. Stand facing each other and push each other gently. You will both move apart. For your push, there is an equal push in the opposite direction – Newton's third law.

Faster or Slower

All around us things are not only moving but also either accelerating – speeding up – or decelerating – slowing down. Very few things remain at the same speed for long. They also change direction, and even go round and round in circles. All because of a number of different forces at work.

Speeding up

How much something accelerates, or decelerates, depends on two things: the size – or the mass – of the object, and the size of the forces pushing or pulling it. Hit a golf ball – low mass – with a golf club and it could travel a hundred metres or more. Hit a football – higher mass – with the same golf club – same force – and it won't go very far. And the harder you hit the ball, the faster it will travel and the further it will go before it comes back down to the ground.

Speed measures the rate at which something moves – or the distance travelled by an object in a set time. If you walk 6 km (distance) in one hour (time), your speed is 6 kmh (kilometres per hour). Velocity depends on speed and direction. So, if you're feeling energetic and walk round an athletics track at 6 kmh, your velocity changes as you go round the bends, but your speed stays the same.

When a space rocket takes off, the rocket's engines provide powerful thrust, or force, and the rocket accelerates. As the fuel for the engines is used up, the rocket's mass decreases and it accelerates further.

18

Try this!

Bouncing the ball

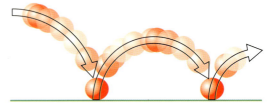

You will need a ball for this – a tennis ball or a football will do. Bounce the ball on the ground. As the ball moves downwards it accelerates, partly because of the force applied by your hand, and partly because of gravity pulling it down. When it hits the ground, its velocity is briefly zero before it bounces upwards. As it moves upwards it accelerates at first, but then decelerates until it reaches the top of the bounce when its velocity is zero. If you let the ball bounce without hitting it, it bounces less high each time because it gradually loses energy – to provide the force to push it back up again.

Gripping stuff

Kick a football along the ground and it won't keep going for ever (fortunately, otherwise you'd keep having to buy new balls). That's because of a force called friction which occurs whenever two surfaces touch each other. It slows down the movement of objects sliding over each other. Friction between the ground and the ball slows it down and eventually brings it to a stop. The more two objects are pressed together, the more friction there is.

Things are being slowed down by friction all around us, and always have been. That can be a nuisance sometimes, but friction is not all bad. In fact, it's vital. Without it, your shoes would not grip the ground so you wouldn't be able to walk anywhere. Worst of all you wouldn't be able to pick up anything – including sweets – with your fingers.

You move faster on a water slide than on an ordinary slide because the water reduces the friction between you and the slide.

 **Sliding board**

You will need a large, smooth wooden board – a chopping board will do – a toy wooden brick, a strip of felt and a strip of sandpaper. Put the brick on to one end of the board. Slowly lift that end until the brick starts to slide down the slope. Now put the felt on the board. Hold it in place while you put the brick on top and lift the board again. Do you have to lift it higher this time? Remove the felt and do the same using the sandpaper. How high do you have to lift it this time?

Amazing fact

Returning spacecraft glow red hot as they re-enter the Earth's atmosphere because of friction between themselves and molecules in the air.

Both felt and sandpaper – especially sandpaper – increase friction between the brick and the wood, so you have to raise the board higher to overcome friction and get the weight to move. Can you think of a way of reducing the friction?

Down to Earth

Ever wondered why you always rapidly come back down when you jump in the air? It's because of a force called gravity, the force of attraction between any two bodies of matter. But it is only strong if something has a large mass, like a planet. Earth's gravity keeps us firmly on the ground and stops us flying off into space.

Ground rules

Italian scientist Galileo Galilei was the first to get to grips with gravity. For centuries people believed that objects fell to the ground because they were 'seeking their natural places' and that heavier objects fell faster than lighter ones. Galileo didn't think this was true. He suggested that all objects fell to the ground in the same time, and that he could prove it by dropping balls of different weights off the leaning tower of Pisa. Why? Because gravity pulls all freely falling objects to the ground with the same acceleration regardless of their weight.

Ideas about gravity were really knocked into shape by Isaac Newton. Newton was at his country home in Lincolnshire in 1665, avoiding the plague which happened to be doing the rounds at the

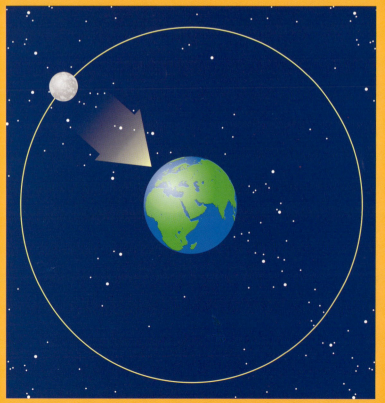

time. Sitting in his garden, he noticed an apple falling to the ground from a tree and suddenly had a gravitational inspiration. He realized that all objects are drawn to the centre of other objects, so the apple is pulled towards the centre of the Earth. The same force – gravity – also keeps the Moon in orbit around the Earth, and the planets in orbit around the Sun. He went on to show that the greater the mass of the object, the greater its gravitational pull, explaining why you keep your feet on the ground.

The Earth's mass is greater than the Moon's, so the Earth's gravity keeps the Moon in orbit and stops it from floating off into space.

Did you know?

You would weigh less on the Moon (if you could get there) than you do on Earth. Why? Your weight depends on the force of gravity pulling on your mass. Of course, wherever you are, you have the same mass. But on the Moon, gravity is just one-sixth that on Earth, so your weight is also one-sixth of what normally appears on the bathroom scales. On the other hand, if you were on the planet Jupiter (which is 318 times heavier than Earth) you would have problems moving because you would be over two and a half times heavier than you are on Earth.

Try this!

Increasing drag

Take a model figure (not a china one!) and stand on a chair. Throw the figure gently in the air. It should fall pretty quickly, thanks to gravity. Now make a parachute for the figure. Take a plastic carrier bag and cut a large square out of one side of it. Tie a 50cm-long cotton thread to each corner of the square, and tie the other ends to the arms of the figure. Get back on to the chair. Gently scrunch together the parachute and the figure, then throw it as you did before. This time the figure falls rapidly until the parachute opens. Drag – friction – between the parachute and the air resists the pull of gravity so that the figure drops more slowly.

21

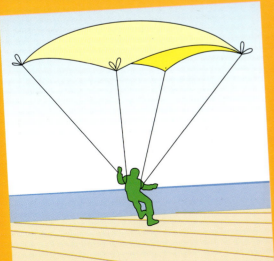

Galileo's test

You don't need to go to Pisa to do this experiment. Take two coins, one larger and heavier than the other. Stand on a chair, hold one coin in each hand, and stretch your arms out in front of you. Drop the coins at the same time and watch them fall – they should hit the floor at the same time. Now try using a coin and a ball of cottonwool. Surprised at the result? You shouldn't be!

Springy and Stretchy

Have you ever seen someone do a bungee jump? They leap off a bridge or tower tethered to a bungee rope. Just a hair's breadth from the water or ground, they come to a halt – or zero velocity – and then bounce upwards. The reason that they don't come to a rather nasty end is because the bungee rope is not an ordinary rope. It is made of elastic materials – materials that can be stretched or squashed, but will return to their original shape.

Changing shape

Forces make things move but they can also change their shape. Some materials, like clay, change their shape and stay changed, which is a good thing if you like pottery or sculpture. Other things are elastic because they change and then 'bounce back' to their original shape or size. Balloons and rubber bands are elastic but so are some metals – when they are in a particular form, that is. Some metals can be drawn out into a fine wire and coiled to make a spring. English scientist and inventor Robert Hooke (1635–1703) was the first person to discover how elastic things stretched. He showed that the amount many elastic materials stretched depended on the force applied to them. Hang a weight on a spring and it stretches a certain amount. Hang twice the weight on it and it stretches twice as far. That is Hooke's Law. However, elastic materials can only be stretched so far until they reach their 'elastic limit', a bit like a point of no return. Beyond this, they will not return to their normal size or they will just snap.

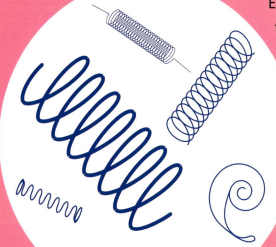

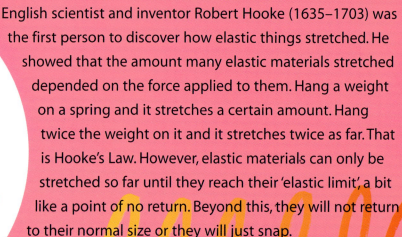

Springs come in all shapes and sizes, depending on their use.

22

Did you know?

Elasticity plays a part in getting blood around your body. Arteries are the blood vessels – tubes – that carry blood from your heart to your ears, toes, liver and everywhere else. Inside the wall of each artery are layers of elastic tissue. Every time your heart beats it sends a great surge of blood along the arteries and their walls bulge outwards, thanks to the elastic tissue. Then a split-second later – also thanks to the elastic tissue – they recoil or bounce back. Bulging makes sure the arteries don't explode as blood flows through them, and recoil keeps blood flowing in a nice smooth fashion. You can feel the bulge and recoil in places – like your wrist – where arteries travel near the surface and over a bone. It's called a pulse.

Try this! A look at Hooke

Draw a spiral shape on a piece of paper and then cut it out by going round and round the spiral until you get to the centre. Now you have a paper spring. Stick one end of the spring to the edge of a table with sticky tape. Put a paper clip on the other end and let go. How far does the spring stretch? What happens when you take the clip off again? Try this with two, three and more paper clips. See what happens if you make your spring from different materials – try card, or a tissue.

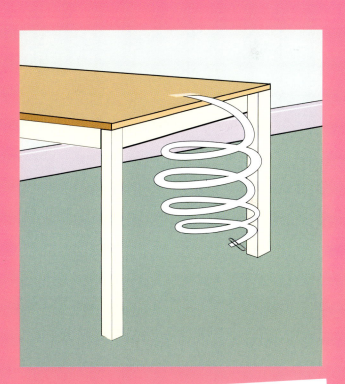

23

Try this! Elastic energy

Take a wide rubber band and hold it against your cheek. It should feel cool. Now quickly stretch the rubber band and then immediately put it against your cheek again. Be prepared for something amazing. It should feel warm. Why? Because when you stretched the rubber band it briefly stored energy from the force that had stretched it. Most of that energy gives it the zip needed to spring back into shape when you let go. But some energy is lost – this always happens – as heat, and that's what warms up the rubber band.

Flying and Floating

Gravity keeps things on the ground so how is it that birds, bats and jets manage to defy gravity and sail through the air? And how can a huge ocean liner sail on the ocean when a stone sinks as soon as it hits the water? It all comes down to a combination of forces. As scientists have discovered how these forces work, things that seemed impossible have become part of our everyday lives. Some discoveries were made in the most unexpected places …

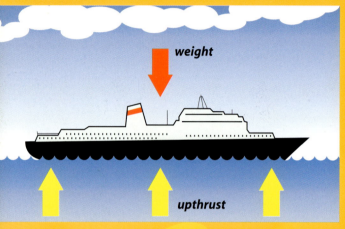

weight

upthrust

Bath time discovery

The brilliant Greek physicist, maths expert and inventor Archimedes (287–212 BC) had his flash of inspiration while taking a bath. As he sank into the tub, he noticed the water level rising. He was so excited that he leapt out of the tub and ran through the streets shouting 'Eureka' ('I've found it' in Greek). Archimedes realized that an object that is placed in water – his body or anything else – displaces, or pushes aside, some of the water. He suggested that the water pushes back against the object with an upward force – called upthrust – that is equal to the weight of water the object displaces. If the upthrust is equal to the object's weight, it will float. But if the upthrust is less than the object's weight, it sinks (like a stone!).

Whether something sinks or floats also depends on its density (how much matter is packed into it, or the weight of an object for its size). A table-tennis ball is very light for its size, and has a low density, so it floats. A golf ball is about the same size but much heavier, so it sinks. A huge ocean liner floats because it has a low density and displaces enough water to provide a large upthrust.

Sink or swim

Try this!

You will need a large plastic bowl, a large piece of modelling clay and a pen. Fill the bowl three-quarters full with water. Roll the modelling clay into a ball and put it in the water. Use the pen to mark the new level of water on the side of the bowl. Remove the clay from the water and pat it dry. Mould it into the shape of a boat with tall sides. Carefully put it back in the water. It should float because now – like real ships – it contains air and is less dense. Check the new water level. It will be higher than the first time, because your 'boat' has displaced more water, so the upthrust is greater.

A historic moment in 1903 – the Wright brothers showed that powered flight was possible.

Up, up and away

A few hundred years ago, people did not believe it was possible for a machine with an engine to fly. Two Americans, Orville and Wilbur Wright, proved them wrong. In 1903, after watching how birds controlled their flight, they built their own flying machine – the Flyer No. 1 – and took it to Kitty Hawk sand flats, North Carolina, to try it out. After a few false starts, on 17 December 1903, Orville Wright actually flew. Not for long (12 seconds) and not very far (36.5m) and not very high (3m), but he did fly. This was a historic moment. Powered flight was possible.

So, how do aircraft – the Flyer or a jumbo jet – actually stay airborne? An aircraft's wing is curved on top and flat underneath. When the wing moves forward, air rushes faster over the top than underneath it. This makes air pressure greater below the wing than above it, so it pushes the wing upwards. This upward force is called lift. If lift is greater than the weight of the plane – pulled downwards by the force of gravity – the plane has to go upwards. Pushing the plane forwards – so that air flows over the wing – is the force called

Did you know?

A bird's wing is curved in the same sort of shape seen in aircraft wings. Obviously birds don't have propellers or jets. For them, forward thrust comes from flapping their wings.

25

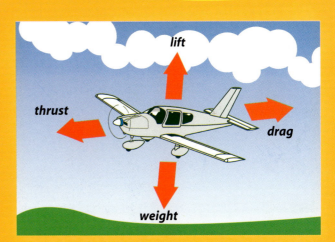

thrust, provided by propellers or jets. This has to overcome a fourth force called drag – the friction caused as the plane rubs against the air. If thrust is greater than drag, and lift is greater than weight, it's up, up and away.

Under Pressure

Which would you choose – someone stepping on your foot with the heel of a flat shoe, or with the heel of a stiletto sandal? If you're sensible you would choose the flat heel. Why? Because the pressure – and the pain – would be far less. Pressure is the amount of force pushing on a particular area. Increase the area and the pressure decreases. That's why it's easier to move over snow without sinking on skis – they have a larger area – than on foot – smaller area. Actually, we are constantly under pressure . . .

Snow shoes spread your weight over a larger area, so you don't sink into the snow.

Air pressure

Believe it or not, the air presses on you all the time, in the same way you press on the ground with your feet. You can't actually feel it, but it does exist. For proof, look no further than Otto von Guericke (1602–1686). He was studying the pressure of the atmosphere, and decided to make a vacuum – an empty space where there's no air and, consequently, no air pressure.

Von Guericke made a vacuum pump that could pump the air out of sealed structures. For his experiment, he used two copper hemispheres – cup shapes – that fitted together with an airtight seal to make a hollow sphere. In 1654, in front of an audience, he pumped the air out of the sphere. He then instructed 50 fit young men – 25 to each hemisphere – to take part in a tug-of-war to pull them apart. They failed. He then tried to separate the hemispheres with two teams of horses, eight in each team. They failed as well. This atmospheric pressure, he reasoned, must be pretty powerful to push the two hemispheres together so strongly. Finally, he turned a tap to let air back into the sphere. With that, the two hemispheres simply fell apart, once the air pressure inside equalled the air pressure outside.

Amazing fact

If you were suddenly transported to the deepest part of the ocean, you would immediately be squashed flat! The water would push down on you with a pressure equivalent to seven elephants balanced on a small plate. That's about 1,000 times the pressure at sea level.

Deep sea divers have to wear special diving suits to protect them from the huge pressure of the water above them.

Try this!

Water spout

You will need a large (1.5 or 2 litre), empty plastic bottle, a nail and a large dish. Ask an adult to cut the top off the bottle, and to use the nail to make four small holes at equal distances up one side. Put the plastic cylinder (that's what it is now) in the dish. Now fill a jug with water. Put your fingers over the holes in the cylinder and ask the adult or a friend to fill it with the water from the jug. Then take your fingers away. Water will shoot out through all the holes, but it squirts furthest from the bottom hole than from the top. That's because water pressure is greater at the bottom – because of the greater weight, or force, of water above it – than at the top.

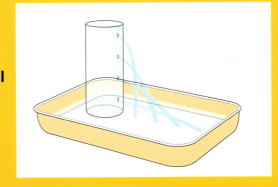

27

Did you know?

▶▶ Air pressure is the result of all the molecules in the atmosphere – oxygen, nitrogen and many others – buzzing around, constantly bombarding you. The pressure from them is so great that you would be crushed if it wasn't for the fact that liquids inside your body push outwards with the same pressure as the air pushes inwards.

▶▶ Air pressure decreases as you go higher. On the highest mountains, air pressure is about half that at sea level. That means your lungs have to work harder to breathe air in.

Making Life Easier

Here's a knotty problem for you. You've been presented with a large tin of paint and have been asked to get the lid off. How would you do it? However much you tug with your fingernails, you wouldn't be able to shift it. But where there's a will, there's a way. Take a long screwdriver, and place the flat tip just under the rim of the lid, so the bit just behind it rests on the edge of the can. Now gently push downwards on the handle and – voilà – the lid comes off. Congratulations. You have used a simple machine.

Simple machines

Machines such as levers, pulleys, gears, wheels and axles, inclined planes and screws are a way of using force in the right place to get a job done. They enable you to do things you couldn't do on your own by exerting more force than you can. A force called the effort applied to one part of the machine overcomes an opposing force called the load in another part of the machine.

● **Lever** – any bar resting on a point called a fulcrum used to push or pull a load up by magnifying the effort (force provided by you or another machine). The further away from the fulcrum that the effort is applied, the more it is magnified. There are three types of lever.

Type 1 – like a crowbar. The fulcrum is always somewhere between the effort and the load.

Type 2 – like a wheelbarrow. The load lies between the effort and the fulcrum.

Type 3 – like a hammer. The effort is between the fulcrum and the load.

● **Pulley** – one or more grooved wheels hung off the ground with rope around the wheel making it easier to lift heavy objects.

● **Gears** – small and large interlocked wheels with teeth that pass on and magnify force, as in a bicycle.

● **Inclined plane** – a slope that makes it easier to move objects to a higher level. Rolling something up a ramp is easier than lifting it and requires less force. A screw is simply a shaft with an inclined plane wrapped around it that makes it easier to push into wood. Or, in the case of a corkscrew, into a cork!

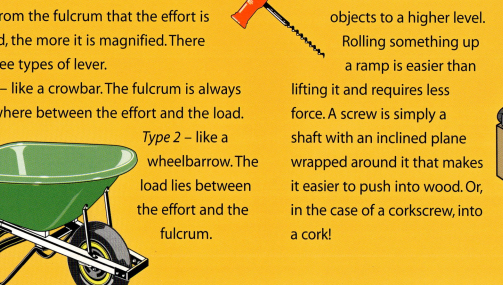

Complex machines, such as a combine harvester, can do several things at the same time.

Did you know?

▶▶ Ancient Greek physicist and naked exhibitionist (see page 24) Archimedes said 'Give me a lever long enough and a place to stand, and I could move the world'. He realized that levers – and pulleys as well – magnified a force and he put his knowledge to practical use.

▶▶ There's a whole set of levers inside your body! Muscles (effort) pull on bones (load) across joints (fulcrums) to move your body.

Amazing fact

In 1822 French inventor Nicolas Appert came up with the idea of canning as a means of keeping food fresh. But canned food did not really take off at first. Why? Because there was no such thing as a can opener. This simple machine wasn't invented until 1855.

29

Try this!

Ease of opening

First of all, half open a door (make sure no one else is around so the door doesn't painfully

transfer its momentum to your head when they suddenly push it). With two fingers, push against the door about 3cm from its hinges. Now go to the other edge of the door (the handle edge) and again push with two fingers about 3cm from the edge. Was it easier to push the door on the hinge edge or the handle edge? It should have been the handle edge. The door works like a lever. The hinges provide the fulcrum, the door's weight the load, and your fingers the effort. The further away the effort is applied from the fulcrum, the more the force is magnified (so it's easier to open).

Changed Lives

Heat, light, entertainment, communication – since the late 19th century, electricity has dramatically changed our lives. No longer do you have to read by candlelight (except during a power cut) or cook over a fire (unless burning sausages on the barbecue). You can watch films on television, microwave a meal in a few minutes, access the Internet on your computer, or talk to a friend on a mobile phone, all thanks to early pioneers like Michael Faraday.

Into the home

Electricity is produced at power stations. Inside their generators, massive magnets spin between huge coils of wire. As the magnets spin between the coils, electricity flows in the wires. But what makes them spin? Thermal power stations use heat to make steam, and the steam drives a turbine (a set of blades that turn on an axle) which turns the magnets. The heat is usually produced by burning oil, coal, or gas. Nuclear power stations also use heat energy to drive generators, but it is released from radioactive materials. Hydroelectric power stations use water gushing in from dams to turn the turbines. Tidal power also uses water – the movement of the tides.

Wind power uses the energy of the wind to turn giant propellers linked to generators, set on the top of tall towers, in naturally windy places, like near the coast.

Did you know?

Coal, oil, and gas were formed underground over millions of years. Lots of countries use them to generate electricity, but they release polluting carbon dioxide into the air – one of the main causes of global warming. Also, they are going to run out in the next few hundred years. That is why more and more people are in favour of renewable energy sources, like hydroelectric and wind power, that won't run out and don't cause pollution.

Amazing fact

Photovoltaic (solar) cells convert sunlight energy directly into electricity. Scientists are investigating the possibilities of using solar power to provide energy in all our homes.

Glossary

Acceleration
The rate of the change in an object's velocity.

Circuit
A path around which an electric current can flow. If the circuit is broken, current will not flow.

Commutator
A device that changes the direction of electric current in a circuit.

Conductor
Something that lets electricity or heat pass through.

Drag
A force that acts on an object moving through air or water.

Electrode
Something that collects or releases electrons in an electric circuit. It is usually a piece of metal or another conductor.

Electrolyte
A liquid that conducts electricity.

Friction
The force between surfaces that are touching.

Gravity
The force that pulls on everything, especially down towards the centre of the Earth.

Insulator
Something that does not let electricity or heat pass through.

Mass
The amount of matter (or 'stuff') in an object.

Newton meter
A spring balance used to measure force. Force is measured in newtons.

Orbit
The path of one body, such as a planet, around another body.

Speed
The rate at which an object moves or the distance travelled by an object in a set time.

Upthrust
The force pushing up on an object in water or air or on a solid surface.

Vacuum
Where there is no air.

Velocity
The speed of an object in a particular direction.

Weight
The force pulling down on something because of gravity.

Index